JOHN LOCKE

Champion of Modern Democracy

PHILOSOPHERS OF
THE ENLIGHTENMENT™

JOHN LOCKE | Champion of Modern Democracy

Graham Faiella

rosen
central™

The Rosen Publishing Group, Inc., New York

For Freedom, and her sisters, Liberty and Happiness

Published in 2006 by The Rosen Publishing Group, Inc.
29 East 21st Street, New York, NY 10010

First Edition

Library of Congress Cataloging-in-Publication Data

Faiella, Graham.
John Locke: champion of modern democracy / by Graham Faiella.—
1st ed.
    p. cm.—(Philosophers of the Enlightenment)
Includes bibliographical references and index.
ISBN 1-4042-0420-2 (library binding: alk. paper)
1. Locke, John, 1632–1704.
I. Title. II. Series.
B1297.F35 2005
192—dc22

                                                      2004030625

Manufactured in Malaysia

On the cover: Inset: Seventeenth-century oil painting of John Locke; Background: A painting depicting the arrival of William of Orange in London during the Glorious Revolution, which Locke supported. His view that governments did not possess absolute power over their subjects had greater impact throughout the rest of Europe and in America than it did in his native England.

CONTENTS

Introduction 7

CHAPTER 1 Europe and England in the
Seventeenth Century 13

CHAPTER 2 John Locke: His Life 24

CHAPTER 3 *An Essay Concerning Human
Understanding* and Other Works 32

CHAPTER 4 Influences on Locke 53

CHAPTER 5 The Meaning of Locke's Philosophy 70

CHAPTER 6 The Influence and Importance
of Locke's Ideas 84

Timeline 98

Glossary 100

For More Information 102

For Further Reading 104

Bibliography 106

Index 108

SCIENCE AND THE ENLIGHTENMENT

- • Leading academic centers
- □ Observatories

Uppsala
Stockholm
SCOTLAND
Smith
Watt
Glasgow
Edinburgh
Copenhagen
Königsberg
Kant
Danzig
ENGLAND
Bacon
Boyle
Hume
Locke
Newton
Cambridge
Halle
Berlin
Toruń
Copernicus
London
Amsterdam
Göttingen
Van Leeuwenhoek
Leipzig
Greenwich □
Spinoza
Leibniz
Paris
Descartes
Diderot
Montesquieu
Rousseau
Voltaire
Strasbourg
Padua
Venice
Galileo
Turin
Bologna
Rome
Madrid
Naples

0   250   500
MILES

This map of Europe shows the major academic centers and scientific observatories during the seventeenth and eighteenth centuries. The scientific revolution of the seventeenth century, which advanced the understanding of nature, was a major influence on the Enlightenment philosophers, who reasoned that, like nature, people and society could be objects of scientific study. Their inquiries and philosophies gave birth to what today are called the social sciences.

INTRODUCTION

The eighteenth century is known as the Enlightenment because of the revolutionary work of a group of writers who challenged the prevailing view of government, science, and religion. These writers, called philosophes, championed the human capacity to reason. Over time, they influenced a shift in their societies away from religious superstition and the concept of the divine right of kings toward human rationality and the idea that every person is born with certain basic rights.

The Enlightenment reached its maturity during the mid- to late eighteenth century. However, the movement began in the late seventeenth century following a flurry of scientific discoveries that disproved dominant religious explanations of the physical universe. John Locke was one of the major players in this new intellectual movement.

John Locke was perhaps the most widely read political philosopher during the eighteenth century. Many historians mark the beginning of the Enlightenment with the publication of his *An Essay Concerning Human Understanding* in 1690.

His writings were a driving influence among the later, more celebrated Enlightenment figures and a key source of inspiration in the development of modern democracy.

About a year before he died, John Locke wrote a letter to his young friend Anthony Collins. In the letter, dated November 17, 1703, Locke wrote, "If I have anything to boast of, it is that I sincerely love and seek truth with indifferency [no matter] whom it pleases or displeases."

For Locke, truth was the guiding light of human life. Whatever a person discovered to be "true" was found by his or her power of reasoning. Reason was the supreme authority for all Enlightenment philosophers. Locke believed that individuals should be free to seek their own truths in their own way, with their own minds, and with respect for the right of others to do so as well. His views on equality and toleration were based on respect for individuals' freedom to be guided by reason toward their own enlightenment. Toleration was the measure of a person's respect for others. Tolerant people recognized that everyone had weaknesses. No one, not even kings, had the power of absolute authority over others.

If all of Locke's philosophy could be distilled into a single concept, it would be that the unique human faculty of reason—our ability to make moral judgments—gives us the ability to decide our own destiny.

English historian Lord Peter King wrote of Locke in 1884:

> Reason was his rule and guide in everything; toleration was his text [guidebook]; and he abhorred those . . . who pervert that divine precept [principle], which teaches to promote peace on earth, and good-will towards man.

Locke lived through turbulent times in seventeenth-century England: violent conflicts between the English parliament and the monarchy, religious conflict and persecution, the abolition and later restoration of the monarchy, and wars with France and Spain. It was a time when many human freedoms that we take for granted today were restricted or abused by tyrannical royal power. The seventeenth century was also, however, a century of discovery and scientific revolution. The discoveries of scientists such as Galileo Galilei (1564–1642), Isaac Newton (1642–1727), and Robert Boyle (1627–1691) led to new, revolutionary ways of looking at nature. Locke himself studied medicine and was a man of science. He believed that a knowledge of science taught a person how to think and make the best use of his or her intellect.

In a 1697 letter to the Earl of Peterborough, he wrote:

> When a man has got an entrance into any of the sciences, it will be time then to depend on himself, and rely upon his own understanding, and exercise his own faculties, which is the only way to improvement and mastery.

Locke writes in the "Epistle to the Reader," the preface to his greatest work, *An Essay Concerning Human Understanding*, that "philosophy . . . is nothing but the true knowledge of things." Whether scientific or philosophical, the pursuit of knowledge toward the discovery of truth was, for Locke, the greatest possible expression of human liberty and happiness. For Locke, as for other Enlightenment thinkers, the unique capacity for humans to reason was the candle that illuminated the path toward truth, liberty, and happiness. Anything not guided by reason, as Locke says in the "Epistle to the Reader," was "rubbish that lies in the way to knowledge."

This seventeenth-century German engraving depicts a scholar studying the stars and the Milky Way. The century saw an outburst of scientific inquiry, invention, and discovery that challenged the existing, dominant religious theories on the nature of the world.

Today, historians regard Locke as a key figure in the history of philosophy. The United States and other democracies around the world are indebted to his two major works, *An Essay Concerning Human Understanding* and *Two Treatises of Government*, for their ideas on basic human rights, representative government, and separation between church and state. These ideas were not commonplace in the world into which Locke was born.

EUROPE AND ENGLAND IN THE SEVENTEENTH CENTURY

By the early 1600s, Europe was divided by religion. Spain and France were Catholic. The main Protestant powers were England, Germany (which was actually a group of territories in the Holy Roman Empire and not a unified German state), and northern Holland. At that time Holland was the main member of the United Provinces of the Netherlands and was ruled by Spain. Northern Holland opposed Spanish rule and was Protestant. The south, which is now Belgium, was controlled by Spain and was mainly Catholic. Catholic Italy, which would not become a unified country until 1860, was composed of separate independent city-states in the seventeenth century. Alliances among European

Entitled *A Village Street with Peasants and Travelers, A Canal Beyond*, this oil painting by Jan Brueghel the Younger presents a view of peasant life in seventeenth-century Europe. Peasant life was dominated by poverty, demanding agricultural labor, and high taxes. Good harvests were celebrated with fairs; poor harvests brought hunger and famine, which made peasants vulnerable to disease.

powers were made, and wars were waged on the basis of religion or dynastic power. The Thirty Years' War (1618–1648) was mainly a religious conflict between Catholic and Protestant nations.

HOLLAND

Holland had a special position in Europe in the seventeenth century. The little country had become prosperous from international trade. Prosperity fed cultural and scientific achievements. Antoni van Leeuwenhoek (1632–1723) and Jan Swammerdam (1637–1680) were pioneers in scientific discoveries by observations with the microscope. The physicist Christian Huygens (1629–1695), from Amsterdam, developed significant theories and made important discoveries in mathematics, astronomy, and physics. These included the development of the advanced pendulum clock, which allowed for a more accurate measurement of time. Locke called him "the great Huygenius" in the "Epistle to the Reader." One of the most important philosophers of the twentieth century, Bertrand Russell (1872–1970), wrote of Holland in his *History of Western Philosophy*:

> It is impossible to exaggerate the importance of Holland in the seventeenth century, as the one country where there was freedom of speculation [debate] . . . Early liberalism was a product of England and Holland . . . It stood for religious toleration; it was Protestant . . . it regarded the wars of religion as silly. It . . . favoured the rising middle class rather than the monarchy and the aristocracy; it had immense respect for the rights of property, especially when accumulated by the labours of the individual . . . There was a belief . . .

Christian Huygens made important contributions to the fields of physics, mathematics, mechanics, and astronomy during the seventeenth century. He discovered Titan, Saturn's largest moon, invented the pendulum clock, and made significant improvements to the telescope. His writings were very influential throughout Europe's scientific communities. The seventeenth-century pendulum clock shown in the inset was built by Johannes van Ceulen, based on Huygens's design.

that all men are born equal, and that their subsequent inequality is a product of circumstances. This led to a great emphasis on the importance of education . . .

In short, Holland had all the qualities that Locke professed in his philosophy. Although strictly Protestant, Holland was a haven of toleration for political and religious exiles from other European countries. Locke spent five years there between 1683 and 1688. The great French philosopher René Descartes (1596–1650) lived there between 1629 and 1649. The Dutch Jewish philosopher Benedict de Spinoza (1632–1677) was born in Amsterdam to a Portuguese family that had fled to Holland to escape persecution during the Spanish Inquisition. The future English king Charles II (1630–1685) hid in Holland when the English Civil War started going badly for his Royalist forces.

ENGLAND

As in the rest of Europe, religious conflict ran rampant in England during the seventeenth century. The Pilgrims, who were Puritans, sailed for America on the *Mayflower* to escape religious persecution a dozen years before Locke's birth. Puritans were hard-core English Protestants who opposed the Church of England, which they regarded as corrupt. They also wanted to rid the church of the pomp, ceremonies, and procedures that reflected its origins in the Roman Catholic Church.

Locke was born during the reign of Charles I (1625–1649). Charles was the first English king to be raised within the Protestant Church of England. However, he was generally thought to support Catholicism. His marriage to Henrietta Maria, a French Catholic princess, helped to further this view. England at the time was very anti-Catholic. Charles also ruled like a dictator. He virtually ignored Parliament. The hostility between Charles and Parliament, the Puritans' grievances against him, and his tyrannical abuse of royal power led to the English Civil War (1642–1651). (Locke's father, a Puritan and a lawyer, fought on the side of Parliament against the king's supporters, the Royalists.) Toward the end of the war, Charles I was convicted of treason. He was executed in London on January 30, 1649.

A month after King Charles's execution, Parliament abolished the monarchy, the House of Lords (the part of Parliament where the nobility sat), and the Church of England. Between 1649 and 1653, England was a commonwealth ruled by a council of

This portrait of Charles I shows the English king immediately before his execution on January 30, 1649, by order of Parliament. The portrayal of the king with uplifted hands suggests the Royalist view that the king was a martyr.

state. In 1653, it became a so-called protectorate. Oliver Cromwell (1599–1658), leader of the English army, was lord protector. After Cromwell died, the protectorate was abolished in 1659. Charles I's son became King Charles II. He ruled from 1660 to 1685. The Restoration of the monarchy, as it was called, included the restoration of a full Parliament and the Church of England. However, it also included persecution of Protestants, such as Quakers and Baptists, who were not part of the Church of England.

Charles II leaned even more toward Catholicism than his father did. The Catholic French king Louis XIV (1638–1715) supported him with money and troops. In exchange, Charles II secretly agreed to convert to Catholicism. Most people in England were Protestant, very anti-Catholic, and very anti-French (because France was Catholic). Throughout his reign, Charles II frequently clashed with Parliament. His Catholicism antagonized his subjects. However, Charles II was interested in science and he supported scientific achievement. The Royal Society in London was established during his reign, with the goal of "improving Natural Knowledge." Two notable natural disasters occurred during Charles II's reign: the bubonic plague that spread throughout England in 1665, and the Great Fire of London in 1666.

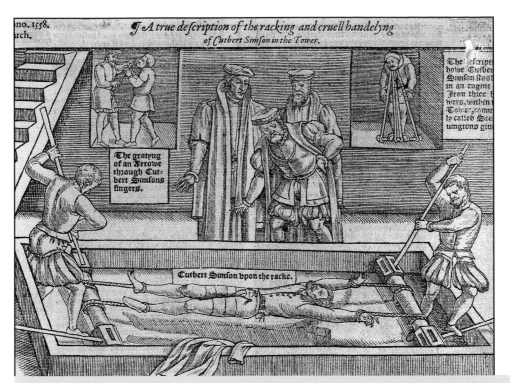

¶ A true description of the racking and cruell handelyng of Cutbert Simson in the Tower.

The grayng of an Arrowe through Cutbert Simsons fingers.

Cutbert Simson vpon the racke.

The description howe Cutbert Simson stood in an engine Iron thrise within the Tower, commonly called Scevingtons gina

Published in John Foxe's *Book of Martyrs* during the sixteenth century, this illustration shows a victim of religious persecution being stretched and tortured on a rack. Well into the eighteenth century, many governments went to great lengths to suppress or purge religious minorities from their societies. Freedom of religion is a rather modern concept that developed during the Enlightenment.

Charles II's younger brother, James, Duke of York (1633–1701), became a Catholic before inheriting the throne as James II in 1685. Like his father, James ignored Parliament during his brief three years on the throne. His son and heir to the throne, also named James, was born in 1688. It was feared that he, too, would be Catholic. For Protestant England, this was too much. The bishop of London and six supporters asked William of Orange (1650–1702), in Holland, who was married to James

William of Orange was the ruler of the Netherlands when English parliamentarians and members of the clergy invited him to invade England and rescue its government from King James II's control. John Locke was supportive of this invasion. Although he wrote *Two Treatises of Government* before the Glorious Revolution, his famous work was widely believed to be a justification of the revolution during the Enlightenment.

II's daughter Mary (1662–1694), to come to England to take over the throne. William arrived and easily overthrew James II in the Glorious Revolution of 1688. William was crowned King William III. He reigned from 1689 to 1702. Mary reigned alongside her husband as Queen Mary II until her death in 1694. During their reign, Protestantism, the Church of England, and Parliament were all restored. Their reign established democratic government by Parliament, which restricted the abuses of royal power that had plagued England since Charles I.

John Locke: His Life

John Locke was born on August 29, 1632, at Wrington, Somerset, in the west of England, to an Anglican Protestant family with Puritan tendencies. His mother died while he was still an infant. His father, also named John, was an attorney. He taught his son the values of hard work, the appreciation of simplicity and moderation, and the love of liberty. In his book *John Locke*, Richard Aaron writes that Locke "would hear his father expound [explain] the doctrine of the rightful sovereignty of the people through its elected Parliament." The influence of his father's devotion to liberty in particular would carry through into Locke's philosophical beliefs.

LOCKE'S EDUCATION

From 1646 to 1651, Locke went to Westminster School in London. In

1652, Locke was elected to a studentship at Christ Church College, Oxford University. (A Christ Church studentship in Locke's time meant a lifetime fellowship for study and research there.) According to Lord Peter King, Locke distinguished himself there, especially among his fellow students, by his talents and learning. The Oxford curriculum was a conventional diet of rhetoric, grammar,

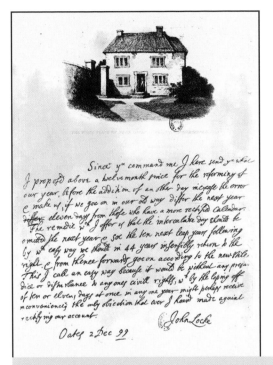

This letter that John Locke wrote on December 2, 1699, includes a drawing of the house in Wrington, Somerset, in which the English philosopher was born. Locke was the first of three sons.

moral philosophy, geometry, and the Greek language based on the teachings of the ancient Greek philosopher Aristotle (384–322 BC). Locke considered the curriculum pedantic and dogmatic, loaded with "obscure terms and useless questions." He studied medicine at Christ Church but never formally became a doctor. Nevertheless, he treated people who came to him with various medical complaints, a practice that earned him the nickname Dr. Locke.

This 1813 engraving shows the library of Christ Church College in Oxford, England, where Locke earned his bachelor of arts degree in 1656, and his master of arts degree in 1658. Locke later lectured in courses in Greek and rhetoric there. In 1663, the university appointed him censor of moral philosophy, a senior disciplinary position.

Locke started to focus on philosophy in the mid-1660s, while he was living in Oxford. He became friends with the scientist Robert Boyle and helped Boyle in his experiments. Boyle played an important role in the early years of the Royal Society, which was established in 1662 by a group of scientists and natural philosophers from London and Oxford. Locke was associated with the Oxford group. He was elected a member of the Royal Society in 1668.

Robert Boyle was one of the leading natural philosophers of the seventeenth century. Natural philosophy is the objective study of nature and the physical universe. Boyle is often referred to as the father of modern chemistry because of his tremendous contributions to the field, including the formulation of the physical law that explains how the pressure and volume of gas are related. He pioneered the scientific method of conducting and reporting controlled experiments that is still the standard today.

THE EARL OF SHAFTESBURY: AN INFLUENTIAL CONNECTION

At Oxford in the summer of 1666, Locke met Lord Ashley (later to become the Earl of Shaftesbury). Lord Ashley was a very influential man in government during Charles II's reign. He and Locke became friends. Ashley invited Locke to join his household in London, to be his personal physician and adviser. Ashley and Locke held similar political views. They believed in a Protestant constitutional monarchy, civil liberty, religious toleration, the rule of Parliament, and economic expansion for England. Locke even helped Ashley draft a constitution for the new American colony of Carolina. It included the freedom of worship for everyone except atheists, who are people who do not believe in the existence of God.

In 1672, Lord Ashley, now the Earl of Shaftesbury, was appointed lord chancellor of England. That year, he established the Council of Trade and Plantations. Locke was secretary of the council for two years until 1675, when he returned to Oxford because the polluted London air aggravated his asthma. Soon thereafter, he traveled to France in search of a climate more suitable to his fragile health. He moved around France for four years.

In France, Locke became friends with intellectuals such as François Bernier (1620–1688). Bernier was the leading expert on the French scientific philosopher Pierre Gassendi (1592–1655), whose work influenced Locke. Locke returned to England in 1680.

Meanwhile, Shaftesbury was getting into a lot of trouble because of his political activities against Charles II. He was imprisoned in the Tower of London twice. In 1682, feeling his life

Born Anthony Ashley Cooper, the first Earl of Shaftesbury was a prominent politician during the mid-seventeenth century. As such, he was a resourceful mentor to John Locke, whom he brought into contact with powerful men and for whom he secured important political appointments.

was in danger, Shaftesbury fled to Holland where he died the next year. Locke felt increasingly threatened because of his close association with Shaftesbury. In late 1683, he, too, fled to Holland. There, Locke became associated with English revolutionaries. He was named on a list of eighty-five traitors wanted by the English government, and his Christ

This engraving portrays King William III entering London on December 18, 1688, following his ascension to the English throne during the Glorious Revolution. He is followed by a procession of coaches and is surrounded by a welcoming crowd. The revolution is called glorious because there was no violence or bloodshed in the exchange of rulers.

Church studentship was taken away from him. According to Lord Peter King,

> William Penn [English Quaker and founder of Pennsylvania (1644–1718)], who enjoyed some degree of favour with James II, offered to obtain from the King the pardon of Locke, who nobly refused to accept a pardon, as being conscious of having [believing he had] committed no crime."

Locke's name was eventually removed from the list of traitors in 1686.

In Holland, Locke formed a small society to discuss and debate various philosophical questions. It met weekly at the members' houses. In addition to these debate sessions, Locke was probably also involved with English revolutionaries in exile in Holland plotting to overthrow James II. Eventually the Dutch leader William of Orange did overthrow James II in the Glorious Revolution of 1688, and became William III. The revolution enabled Locke to return to England. He arrived in the same fleet that brought William's wife, Mary. During William III's reign, Locke contributed to the Toleration Act of 1689, allowing greater religious freedom and toleration. He also helped abolish the Act for the Regulation of Printing, thereby securing freedom of the press.

In 1691, Locke retired to the country to live at Oates in the county of Essex, the home of his friends Sir Francis and Lady Masham. There he engaged in political and philosophical discussions with friends who came to see him. Locke died at Oates on October 28, 1704, with Lady Masham at his bedside. He was buried nearby in the churchyard of the village of High Laver.

AN ESSAY CONCERNING HUMAN UNDERSTANDING AND OTHER WORKS

CHAPTER 3

Locke's best-known work is *An Essay Concerning Human Understanding.* While he lived in London with Lord Ashley, Locke used to meet with friends at Ashley's home to discuss philosophy, politics, and social issues of the day. During one of those meetings he came up with the idea for writing *An Essay Concerning Human Understanding.* In the "Epistle to the Reader," Locke explains the origins of the work:

> Were it fit to trouble thee with the history of this essay, I should tell thee that five or six friends meeting at my chamber, and discoursing on a subject very remote from

Locke began putting his thoughts in writing in the 1660s. Even then, he displayed an appreciation for rationalism and tolerance and a dislike for authoritarianism. The publication of *An Essay Concerning Human Understanding* and *Two Treatises of Government* revealed him to be one of the master thinkers of his era.

this, found themselves quickly at a [standstill] by the difficulties that rose on every side. After we had a while puzzled ourselves without coming any nearer a resolution . . . it came into my thoughts, that we took a wrong course; and that, before we set ourselves upon enquiries of that nature, it was necessary to examine our own abilities, and see what objects our understandings were or were not fitted to deal with. This I proposed to the company [to do] . . .

So, Locke wrote down, as he put it, "some hasty and undigested thoughts" on the subject of the "understanding." He presented these notes at the next meeting of the group. After that, he continued to write about the subject and, "after long periods of neglect, resumed again, as my humour [mood] or occasions permitted." Locke finally completed the work while he was exiled in Holland (1683–1689). After returning to England, he completed three more versions of the essay. The fourth and final version was published when he was retired and living at Oates, in 1700. *An Essay Concerning Human Understanding* was formally condemned by Oxford University in 1702. In a letter to a friend, Locke wrote, "I take what has been done there [Oxford's condemnation of the essay] rather as a recommendation of the book."

THE STRUCTURE OF THE ESSAY

The main body of the essay is written in four books. Each book is divided into chapters. Each chapter is divided into paragraphs, each of which is numbered. In book 1 ("Of Innate Notions"), Locke argues why he rejects the concept of innate (inborn) ideas as the source of human knowledge. In book 2 ("Of Ideas"), he lays out his argument for what he believes is the true source of knowledge, namely, the different kinds of "ideas" received onto the *tabula rasa* ("blank slate") of our mind through our sensory perception of the outside world. Book 3 ("Of Words") is devoted to language and the connection between words and ideas. Locke includes in book 3 one of the most important concepts of his philosophy, namely, the difference between "modes" (thoughts and ideas) and "substances" (physical objects). Book 4 ("Of Knowledge and Opinion") explains his view about what knowledge is and how it is different from beliefs and opinions.

At the very beginning of *An Essay Concerning Human Understanding*, Locke includes a dedication to Thomas Herbert, Earl of Pembroke (1656–1733). Herbert and Locke were friends from the mid-1670s.

AN

ESSAY

CONCERNING

Humane Understanding.

In Four BOOKS.

Quam bellum est velle confiteri potius nescire quod nescias, quam ista effutientem nauseare, atque ipsum sibi displicere! Cic. de Natur. Deor. l. 1.

LONDON:

Printed for *Tho. Basset*, and sold by *Edw. Mory*, at the Sign of the *Three Bibles* in St. *Paul's* Church-Yard.　M DC XC.

This is the title page of the first publication of *An Essay Concerning Human Understanding*. Locke, who prepared the preliminary draft in 1671, took close to twenty years to complete the project. More than any of his other writings, the essay presents the basic principles of Locke's philosophy.

Locke's correspondence with Herbert shows the interest Herbert took in the progress of the essay as Locke worked on it for twenty years or so. The "Epistle to the Reader," which precedes book 1 of the essay, is a sort of preface to the work where Locke explains the origins of the essay and his reasons for writing it. Locke, in his humility, says in the epistle that his task in writing the essay was "to be employed as an under-labourer in clearing [the] ground a little, and removing some of the rubbish that lies in the way of knowledge."

LOCKE'S OBJECTIVES

Locke's main objective in writing *An Essay Concerning Human Understanding* was to set out his theory of the origin, nature, and extent of human knowledge. This branch of philosophy is formally called epistemology. Locke's view was that the source of all knowledge was what a person experienced about the outside world through his or her senses. He believed that the power of reason and the faculty of thought, which produced knowledge, placed humans above all other animals in their ability to dominate nature. He explains:

> Since it is the understanding that sets man
> above the rest of sensible beings, and gives

him all the advantage and dominion which he has over them, it is certainly a subject . . . worth our labour to enquire into . . . This, therefore, being [is] my purpose, to enquire into the original [origins], certainty, and extent of human Knowledge, together with the grounds and degrees of Belief, Opinion, and Assent . . .

Humans' ability to achieve mastery over nature was an important principle of all Enlightenment philosophers. It represented the supremacy of human reason over unreasoned animal instinct. Locke shared this belief, but his aim in writing the essay was more practical. He hoped it would be useful to others. As he writes in the epistle: "I publish this essay with hopes it may be useful to others . . . I shall always have the satisfaction to have aimed sincerely at truth and usefulness . . . " This objective reflects the pragmatic character of Locke. The great British philosopher Bertrand Russell writes in his *History of Western Philosophy* that Locke "is always sensible." According to the English philosopher Gilbert Ryle (1900–1976), in his "Collected Papers" (1971), Russell believed that "no one [that is, no philosopher since Aristotle] ever had Common Sense before John Locke."

LETTER CONCERNING TOLERATION

In 1685, Locke wrote his *Letter Concerning Toleration*, (in Latin, *Epistola de Tolerantia*). It was first published anonymously in English in 1689, because he was still nervous about publishing such controversial liberal ideas. Two later revised *Letters* were published in 1690 and 1692. In a time when religious conflict caused a lot of social disturbance, Locke argued for toleration of different religious views as the basis for a peaceful and civilized society. Church and state, he said, should be separate, so that the state could not impose a particular religion or religious dogma on people.

TWO TREATISES OF GOVERNMENT

In 1690, Locke published *Two Treatises of Government*, which outlines his political philosophy. Locke wrote the first treatise specifically to criticize *Patriarcha; or, The Natural Power of Kings*, a work by the English political philosopher Sir Robert Filmer (1588–1653). In *Patriarcha*, Filmer argues that kings (monarchs) had a divine right to rule. Their absolute power was given to them by God and was, therefore, beyond all human control. In the same way, Filmer argues, fathers always had power

TWO TREATISES
OF
Government:

In the former,

The *false Principles*, and *Foundation*

OF

Sir *ROBERT FILMER*,

And his FOLLOWERS,

ARE

Detected and **Overthrown.**

The latter is an

ESSAY

CONCERNING THE

True Original, Extent, and End

OF

Civil Government.

LONDON,

Printed for *Awnsham Churchill*, at the *Black Swan* in *Ave-Mary-Lane*, by *Amen-Corner*, 1690.

As indicated on this title page from the initial publication of Locke's *Two Treatises of Government*, the first treatise is an attack on the divine rights of kings as championed by Sir Robert Filmer. Locke presents his own political theory in the second treatise.

over their children. This was a very common view in the seventeenth century. Locke argued that Filmer's philosophy was ridiculous, illogical, and unjust. His second treatise explains why rulers do not have absolute God-given powers. He gives his alternative philosophy about how a civil society should function, and what the responsibilities of rulers and subjects are.

The meat of Locke's political philosophy is found in the second treatise, subtitled "An Essay Concerning the True Original, Extent, and End of Civil Government." In the preface to the work, he proclaims that his inspiration was the Glorious Revolution of 1688, when William III came to the throne

> to establish the throne of our great restorer, our present King William [III]; to make good his title, in the consent of the people . . . and to justify to the world [that] the people of England, whose love of their just and natural rights, with their resolution [commitment] to preserve them, saved the nation when it was on the very brink of slavery and ruin.

Locke's political philosophy was based on the concepts of the "state of nature" and "natural law,"

Saint Thomas Aquinas was an Italian priest and philosopher who lived in the thirteenth century. At a time when religious faith and human reason were commonly seen to be at odds, he argued that both were gifts from God. His philosophy is the official philosophy of the Catholic Church today. He was made a saint after his death.

which were derived from medieval times and, in particular, the writings of Saint Thomas Aquinas (1224–1274). Locke defines the state of nature as:

Men [people] living together according to reason, without a common superior on earth, with authority to judge between them.

The key words are "according to reason, without a common superior on earth." Locke believed in the equality of reason, which gave everyone the possibility of freedom to live their own lives. In the "Second Treatise" Locke refers to rich and tyrannical people who "live by another Rule than reason . . . [and] may be destroyed as . . . wild savage beasts." Tyrants, in other words, could legitimately be deposed. Citizens of the community had an obligation to God not to "harm another in his life . . . liberty, or . . . goods [property]." According to Locke, they had the freedom to defend themselves against any attack on their life, liberty, and property, according to the "law of nature" by which the community lived:

> The state of nature has a law of nature to govern it, which obliges every one; and reason, which is that law, teaches all mankind . . . that being all equal and independent, no one ought to harm another in his life, health, liberty, or possessions [property].

To protect against members of society who broke the law, Locke said that people agreed to unite as a community and to "enter into society to make one people, one body politic [political body], under one supreme government." The community would set up a system of justice according to the authority of the majority. People who united as a community gave up some of their personal freedom to achieve a greater freedom, which was peaceful coexistence with others in the community. It was Locke's belief that anyone could withdraw from a community whose government he or she didn't agree with, to "incorporate himself [or herself] into any other community, or . . . to begin a new one."

The main reason why people established a system of government was, according to Locke, to protect their property. He wrote: "The great and chief end of men uniting into commonwealths [communities], and putting themselves under government, is the preservation of their property." Locke defined a citizen as anyone who owned property. Political power was the power to protect a citizen's property:

> Political power I take to be the right of making laws, with penalty of death, and consequently all less penalties for the regulating and preserving of property, and of employing the force of the community in the execution of such laws, and in defence of the commonwealth [community] from foreign injury, and all this only for the public good.

Locke believed in the so-called social contract by which people agreed to come together as a

community. The con-
tract among the citizens
of a community was the
agreement to abide by
the community's rules.
The rights of both the
government and citi-
zens were defined by
the social contract
between them (what we
might call a constitu-
tion). This was Locke's
alternative proposal to
the divine right of
kings to hold absolute
power over his sub-
jects. Citizens had the
right—the obligation,
in fact—to overthrow
those in government
"whenever they [the
government] shall be
so foolish or so wicked,

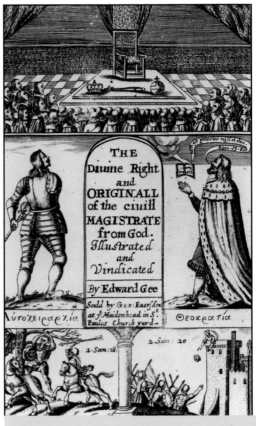

This is the title page from *The Divine Right and Original Magistrate from God*, a seventeenth-century manuscript by Edward Gee that defended the concept of a monarch's divine right to rule. Throughout much of human history, the notion that kings and queens were God's representatives on Earth was unchallenged.

as to lay and carry on designs against the liberties
and properties" of the citizens. Government was
made by the majority. It was always directed
toward the common good of the people who lived

by the rules of the contract. However, Locke believed that people could only be citizens if they owned property. (Slaves, in that sense, were property, not citizens.) Property, Locke said, was whatever a man made his own by the labor he put into making it.

WRITINGS ON EDUCATION

Some Thoughts Concerning Education (1693) was based on letters Locke had written to his friend and distant relative Edward Clarke, while the philosopher was in Holland. Locke dedicated the work to Clarke. The first paragraph of the book clearly states how important Locke thought education was in determining people's character:

> Men's happiness or misery is most part of their own making . . . and I think I may say that of all the men we meet with, nine parts of ten are what they are, good or evil, useful or not, by their education. 'Tis that which makes the great difference in mankind.

Locke believed that there was a right and a wrong way of education. The right way was to cultivate a person's power of reason in the love of truth. Getting into the habit of exercising the "noble faculty" of reason was the main defense against prejudice and what Locke called "ill education." Constant exercise of that "noble faculty" gave one the ability to distinguish "truth from appearances." The right kind of education gave access to knowledge and freedom from prejudice in all its forms. In a later work, *Of the Conduct of the Understanding*, he wrote:

> Every man carries about him a touchstone [guide], if he will make use of it, to distinguish substantial gold from superficial glitterings, [that is,] truth from appearances. And indeed the use and benefit of this touchstone, which is natural reason, is spoiled and lost only by assumed prejudices, overweening presumption, and narrowing our minds. The want [lack] of exercising it [i.e., reason] in the full extent of things intelligible . . . weakens and extinguishes this noble faculty in us.

Once again Locke insists on the power of reason to overcome natural desires. In *Some Thoughts Concerning Education*, Locke wrote that "the Principle of all Vertue [virtue] and Excellency lies in the Power of denying ourselves the Satisfaction of our own Desires, where Reason does not authorize them." Education, he believed, involved a process of learning how to substitute natural desires with the desire for knowledge and truth. The first step in a person's education was learning how to harness the power of reason so that it, and not emotions, was the guiding light toward "Vertue and Excellency." He expanded on this in *Of the Conduct of the Understanding*:

> The business . . . of knowledge is not . . . to perfect a learner in all or any one of the sciences, but to give his mind that freedom, that disposition [inclination], and those habits that may enable him to attain any part of knowledge he shall apply himself to, or stand in need of, in the future course of his life.

Locke believed that education was a process of perfecting the habit of using reason rather than the learning of "all or any one of the sciences" (meaning, any particular academic subject). By learning to use the power of intelligence, he said, a person could overcome natural desires and could "attain any part of knowledge he shall apply himself to, or

DE
L'EDUCATION
DES
ENFANS.

§. I.

LE bonheur, dont on peut jouïr dans ce Monde, se reduit à avoir l'Esprit bien reglé, & le Corps en bonne disposition. Ces deux avantages renferment tous les autres, & l'on peut dire que celui qui les possede tous deux, n'a pas grand' chose à desirer ; au lieu que celui qui est privé de l'un ou de l'autre, n'est guere

Combien il est important de bien élever les Enfans.

A   plus

This is the first page of the 1695 French edition of John Locke's *Some Thoughts Concerning Education*. This work originated from letters Locke wrote to Edward Clarke, a friend who had sought Locke's advice on the education of his children. Clarke was so impressed with the advice that he urged Locke to publish it.

stand [be] in need of, in the future course of his life." That freedom from natural desires (emotions) by submission to reason was a basic principle of Locke's general philosophy. Mastery of a person's self in the pursuit of knowledge was, for Locke, mastery of one's destiny. In *Some Thoughts Concerning Education* he writes:

> He that is a good, a vertuous [virtuous] and able Man [person], must be made so within. And therefore what he is to receive from Education, what is to sway and influence his life, must be something put into him . . . Habits woven into the very Principles of his Nature.

According to Locke, poor education resulted in "truths" that were riveted to the mind from a person's early years, which he or she refused to examine critically later on. Good education meant, for Locke, to get in the habit of using reason to examine critically every rivet of knowledge that became fixed on the mind. Rivets judged to be unsafe (untrue), according to reason, he said, should be pulled out and thrown away. The aim of that habit, "woven into the very Principles of his Nature," was to be a "good and able Man [person]." The only way for a person to achieve that was by "following the Dictates [direction] of that light God has given him [i.e., reason]."

OTHER WORKS

In 1695, *The Reasonableness of Christianity* was published anonymously. Locke's main theme in this work was that true Christianity could be reduced to a small number of principles and practices. Christianity in that minimal form, he said, was rational and logical.

Of the Conduct of the Understanding was Locke's last published work. He intended it to be an added chapter to *An Essay Concerning Human Understanding*, but it became so long that Locke kept it for inclusion in a future edition of *An Essay* or for publication on its own. It was eventually published in 1706, after Locke's death, in *Posthumous Works of Mr. John Locke*, compiled by Lord Peter King, Locke's nephew and heir. *Of the Conduct* is laid out in forty-five sections. Each one discusses a different theme of his philosophy. *Of the Conduct* is a sort of guidebook to the philosophy Locke sets out in *An Essay* and in his other works. It explains how people should manage their intelligence to get the most out of it. Quite a lot of *Conduct* is devoted to the different kinds of human failings that lead to errors and mistakes in the use ("conduct") of our "understanding." *Of the Conduct* focuses on how adults should educate themselves. It complements *Some Thoughts Concerning Education*, which is aimed mainly at the education of children.

INFLUENCES ON LOCKE

CHAPTER 4

The education Locke received at Westminster School and Christ Church College was based on Greek and Roman classical subjects. After graduation from Christ Church, he taught Greek, moral philosophy, and rhetoric at the college. Locke studied the works of Aristotle, in particular, as the most important ancient philosopher. Some basic principles of Locke's philosophy reflect his study of Aristotle. These include the belief that all knowledge is based on the perception of the world through our senses (sensory perception); that philosophical argument requires strict scientific procedure; that there is a difference between the real "essence," or nature, of things, and their "accidental," or perceived, qualities; and that happiness, achieved by the use of intelligence, is the ultimate goal of human life.

Aristotle and other philosophers were influences on but not authorities over Locke's intellect. As much as he absorbed those influences, Locke refused to be governed by them. The only authority he respected was the evidence of his own experience of the world. The writings and ideas of great thinkers in the past were part of that experience, but their teachings were not "knowledge," as defined by Locke. They were simply experiences that his own reason processed to come to his own conclusions about truth. Everything Locke experienced or learned was an influence that advanced his philosophy.

SIR FRANCIS BACON AND INDUCTIVE REASONING

Enlightenment philosophy was grounded on the conviction that the human intellect—reason—could discover truths about nature and the universe. The method of discovering those truths about the outside

The ancient Greek philosopher Aristotle is one of history's greatest thinkers. He developed the science of reasoning known as logic, and his teachings have greatly influenced current thought about how to think rationally. This Roman sculpture of Aristotle, which is housed at the Galleria Spada in Rome, Italy, was patterned after a Greek original.

world could, and should, be used to discover truths about the inner world and nature of human beings. One of the most important influences on Locke's belief in the ways of discovering such truths was the great English statesman and philosopher Sir Francis Bacon (1561–1626). During his life, Bacon achieved high political office as well as the noble titles of Baron Verulam and Viscount of Saint Albans. He is best remembered today for his scientific philosophy, and particularly for his method of inductive reasoning.

In his *Instauratio Magna* (Great Reconstruction; 1909–1914), Bacon proposed first to clear away from a person's mind all prejudices and preconceived ideas. He called such ideas and notions "idols" of the mind. Humans worshiped these "idols" as sacred, believing them, as a matter of trust or faith, to be true, rather than judging them by intelligence and reason. Having cleared away all such idols, Bacon would reconstruct his knowledge of the world based on his direct experience of it. It was Bacon who wrote that "knowledge is power." Bacon's route to both knowledge and power was by the revolutionary method of discovering them for himself.

Before Bacon, philosophers traditionally would first make a hypothetical statement about something ("a square has four sides," for example). Then, by a series of logical proofs, they would deduce whether the proposition is true or false. The evidence for deductive reasoning would be the series of logical steps used to prove the hypothetical statement. Our perception or experience of the outside world (that we could actually see, for example, that a square is not a triangle) is irrelevant.

Deductive reasoning was entirely based on theory, assumptions, and logic. Bacon's method was completely the opposite. He observed something, collected information

Sir Francis Bacon was one of the most important authors and philosophers of sixteenth-century England. Also a high ranking official, he championed the usefulness of science in his writings in part to convince King James I of its advantages.

about it, analyzed the data, and came to a conclusion about the nature of whatever it was he had observed. This is inductive reasoning, a process of scientific observation leading to analysis, experimentation, and, finally, a conclusion. The perception of the external world through our senses would be the evidence for conclusions derived by inductive reasoning. Modern scientific discovery is based on the inductive method. There was no room for theoretical assumptions in Bacon's inductive method. Nor would there be for Locke.

There were other things about Bacon's teachings that greatly impressed Locke. These included his love of truth; his recognition that people lived more by the error of human weakness than by the power of their intellect; that knowledge was not, as Locke said, "for pleasure and vanity only," but "as a spouse, for generation, [bearing] fruit, and comfort"; and that "no pleasure is comparable to the standing upon the vantage-ground of truth." For Bacon, as for Locke, truth was the ultimate virtue. Bacon writes in the essay *Of Truth*:

> The enquiry of truth, which is the love-making or wooing of it; the knowledge of truth, which is the praise of it; and the belief of truth, which is the enjoying of it, is the sovereign good of human nature.

EMPIRICISM

The conventional definition of empiricism is the theory that everything we know originates from what we experience through our five senses (sight, touch, taste, hearing, and smell). This is called sensory experiences. Reason is our intellect, our power to think and make judgments based on our sensory experience. Our intellect's interpretation of our sensory experiences leads to knowledge and truth. Modern science, which is also based on observation and experiment, originates from this philosophical method of reasoning we call empiricism. Francis Bacon's inductive reasoning led to the emergence of empiricism as the basis of Locke's philosophy. Bacon wrote in his work the *Novum Organum*: "Humans, who are the servants and interpreters of nature, can act and understand no further than from what they have observed in . . . nature."

DESCARTES

The French philosopher René Descartes (1596–1650) is often called the founder of modern philosophy. According to Fox Bourne in *The Life of John Locke*, Descartes's influence on Locke is clear from a statement by Lady Masham, Locke's host at Oates:

> The first books, as Mr. Locke himself has told me, which gave him a relish of [enthusiasm for] philosophical things

were those of Descartes. He . . . rejoiced in reading these, because, though he very often differed in opinion from this writer, he yet found that what he said was very intelligible [clear].

Locke disagreed with Descartes's fundamental belief that human beings are born with "innate ideas," inborn principles like seeds that could be cultivated into knowledge. Descartes believed that sensory experiences just distorted the "clear and distinct ideas" that, he said, originated from "innate ideas." One of the first things Locke did in *An Essay Concerning Human Understanding* was to explain why he rejected Descartes's principle of innate ideas:

It is an established opinion amongst some men, that there are in the understanding

This is an illustration from the *Principles of Philosophy* (Principia Philosophiae) by René Descartes *(inset)*, a leading French philosopher and mathematician of the seventeenth century. Widely considered the father of modern philosophy, Descartes was also a prophet of science in that he was the first person to envision using science to control nature.

[mind] certain innate principles . . . stamped upon the mind of man, which the soul receives in its very first being [at birth]; and brings into the world with it . . . I shall set down the reasons, that made me doubt of that opinion.

Locke dedicated an entire chapter of the essay to rejecting Descartes's principle of innate ideas. His argument for rejection led Locke to explain his own thoughts about how the mind arrived at obtaining knowledge which, he said, "I leave to be considered by those, who, with me, dispose themselves to embrace truth, wherever they find it."

Even though Locke believed Descartes was wrong about innate ideas, Descartes's "error" was influential in Locke's development of his own thoughts on the subject. Locke's main criticism of Descartes was that Descartes's scientific philosophy was based more on theory than on "rational experiments and observation." Descartes used the deductive logic of mathematics to arrive at "clear and distinct ideas." Locke, the empiricist, believed that people should study mathematics, as he said, "not so much to make them mathematicians, as to make them reasonable creatures." Mathematics, for Locke, was the best training for people to think more clearly, because the principles of mathematics were clear and concise.

Descartes wrote on the title page of his philosophical work *Discourse on Method* (1637) that he had discovered a new method "for the correct use of reason and for seeking truth in the sciences." In part VI of *Discourse on Method* he claimed that his "completely new science," as he called it, would "make ourselves, as it were, the lords and masters of nature." In Descartes's time, the distinction between science and philosophy was like the difference between the chicken and the egg: they were both a cause and effect of each other.

Locke was strongly influenced by this communion of science and philosophy. Other specific concepts from Descartes that influenced Locke were:

- The revolutionary ambition to overturn old ways of thinking and create a "completely new science"

- The "general rule that the things we conceive [think] very clearly and distinctly are all true" (from *Discourse on Method*) and the rejection of anything not clear and distinct as untrue

- The principle of reductionism, that is, reducing everything to its simplest clear and distinct parts to explain the true nature of things

- The belief that what humans perceive about the outside world is represented in the mind by ideas of those perceptions

- The belief that a person's freedom depends on being true to his or her own thoughts and ideas

- The idea that a person's freedom is diminished by any passions and desires not controlled by reason

PIERRE GASSENDI

Pierre Gassendi (1592–1655), a French scientist and philosopher, was another important influence on Locke. Gassendi's philosophy appealed to Locke in many ways. Gassendi, like Locke, rejected Descartes's concept of innate ideas. He emphasized the inductive method of reasoning and importance of sensory perception. He believed that the harmony of nature was proof of the existence of God. And he believed that the pursuit of moral happiness and avoidance of mental pain was the ultimate goal of all humans.

THE SCIENTIFIC REVOLUTION

Before the seventeenth century, the science of nature was a stewpot of wizardry, magic, and mystery, with a sprinkling of philosophy in a thick sauce of religion. What people thought was knowledge was based mainly on the teachings of Aristotle, which were 1,500 years old. After Aristotle, Christian church teachings based on the Bible, and Catholic dogma in particular, became the standard authority for truth. The scientific revolution of the sixteenth and seventeenth centuries was based on empirical observation. The discoveries were heresy against conventional Aristotelian and Christian beliefs that God created the universe with Earth (and human beings) at its center.

The first important scientific discovery of modern science came from Polish astronomer Nicolaus Copernicus (1473–1543). Copernicus proposed that Earth and the planets revolved around the Sun. Before Copernicus's heliocentric (sun-centered) theory of the universe, the Aristotelian and Christian belief was that the universe and everything in it revolved around Earth. The Danish astronomer Tycho Brahe (1546–1601) advanced Copernicus's theories by recording accurate observations of the

This 1610 engraving by Willem Swanenburgh presents the anatomy hall in the University of Leiden in the Netherlands. The university, which is still in operation, was one of the leading academic centers during the scientific revolution.

stars and planets. The German astronomer Johannes Kepler (1571–1630) was able to use Brahe's astronomical data along with his own to develop new theories about the universe and the nature of light. His textbook on Copernican astronomy influenced seventeenth-century philosophers such as Descartes. The Italian mathematician and astronomer Galileo Galilei (1564–1642) was famous for his construction of an improved version of the telescope, in 1609, that had recently been invented in the Netherlands. Galileo revolutionized natural science and philosophy

Faksimile einer alten Darstellung des Weltgebäudes nach der Vorstellung des Kopernikus
Nach Andreae Cellarii „Harmonia Macrocosmica" vom Jahre 1660

This is a seventeenth-century representation of Copernicus's heliocentric theory of the universe. Copernicus developed his theory about the movements of the planets over thirty years. He died only hours after the publication of *The Revolution of Celestial Spheres* (De Revolutionibus), which contains all his work on astronomy.

with his theories of motion, his use of mathematics to explain natural phenomena, his astronomical observations with his improved telescope, and his confirmation of Copernicus's view of the universe as a heliocentric system.

Sir Isaac Newton, the English physicist and mathematician, was the last but most important figure in seventeenth-century science. Born in the year that

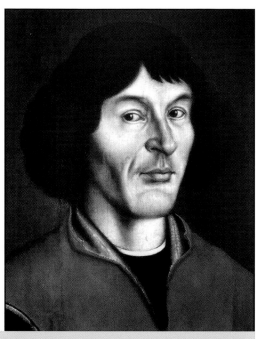

Considered to be the father of modern astronomy, Nicolaus Copernicus changed human understanding of Earth's place in the universe. While working on his groundbreaking theory, as presented in *The Revolution of Celestial Spheres*, he held jobs as a tax collector, judge, physician, and military governor.

Galileo died, Newton was at Cambridge University at the same time Locke was at Oxford. Even though the scientific revolution was well advanced by then, Cambridge and other European universities were still teaching a basically nonscientific, Aristotelian curriculum. On his own, Newton absorbed the works and ideas of contemporary philosophers and scientists such as Descartes, Gassendi, the Copernican astronomers, and the English chemist Robert Boyle. His early contribution to science was in optics and mathematics. His *Principia*, however, published in 1687, signified a dramatic advance in scientific discovery. Newton outlined in *Principia* his universal law of gravitation and philosophy of empirical reasoning. Newton's work became the foundation of modern science.

Locke paid homage to the great scientists of his day. Some of them were friends. Some he knew by reputation. All of them influenced his empirical philosophy as he stood, he seemed to think, in their shadows as "an under-labourer." He wrote in the "Epistle to the Reader":

Sir Isaac Newton is one of the greatest scientists of all time. He made some of the most important discoveries in physics, mathematics, and astronomy, and, in the process, developed a few simple laws that explain many of nature's complicated processes.

But everyone must not hope to be a [Robert] Boyle, or a [Thomas] Sydenham; and in an age that produces such masters, as the great Huygenius, and the incomparable Mr. Newton; 'tis ambition enough to be employed as an under-labourer in clearing ground a little, and removing some of the rubbish that lies in the way of knowledge.

THE MEANING OF LOCKE'S PHILOSOPHY

1
2
3
4
6

CHAPTER 5

Though Locke was a highly educated man, what he understood better than anything was human nature. He had a profound awareness of the division between reason and emotion in the human character. Humans, he believed, were constantly torn between the power of their rational, intellectual nature, and the equal force of their irrational emotions. He understood that humans, like other animals, had what he called natural desires (what we might call animal passions). But humans were unlike other animals, because of their rational power to overcome natural desires. People who lived by brute force and ignorance were inhuman, like animals. Locke considered people to be truly human only when they used the rational part of their nature.

THE IMPORTANCE OF REASON

A rational person was, in Locke's view, a moral person who created moral laws to live by. Morality was, for Locke, the basis of human society. Reason guided the choice a person (or society) made between good and evil. Individuals were responsible for their own decisions. The rational choices people made in their lives determined their freedom, happiness, and virtue.

Locke believed that humans were basically driven by passion, desire, and emotions. He used a lot of ink writing about the ways emotions dictated human behavior. Some of the desires and emotions Locke described were the desire for an easy life; the greed for power; the laziness of accepting other people's opinions as truth; the fear of being an outsider in society and the love of one's own social status; and the fear of criticizing and ultimately rejecting one's own dearly held principles. Emotions and desires are what we might call today the primal instincts of our human nature. (A baby's first action is not to do mathematics, it is to scream.) Locke believed that it was a person's duty to overcome the primal instincts of natural emotions in order to achieve his or her full potential as a rational human being.

Because desire and passion are such powerful forces in humans, Locke believed that people had a

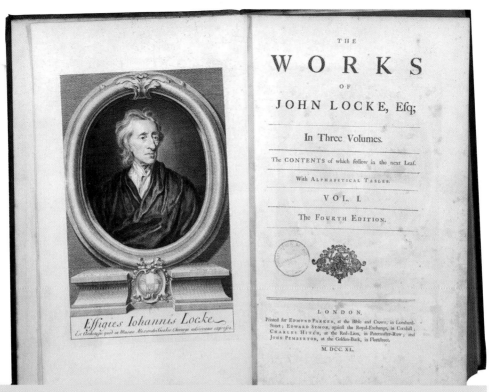

These are the frontispiece and title page of the fourth edition of *The Works of John Locke*, which was published in 1740. By this time, the deceased Locke was one of the most widely read philosophers throughout Europe. His theories about education and government provided ammunition for the philosophers of mid–eighteenth-century France to attack the existing social order, which was dominated by an absolute monarchy and the powerful Catholic Church.

choice about how to respond to their emotions. They could simply act on impulse, or they could act on the basis of reason, having thought about the consequences. The best way for Locke was to think before acting. Using reason to be the judge of any action was, for Locke, the only way to achieve the freedom of self-determination and be the master of one's destiny. Acting on emotion or anything not judged by reason, he believed, was a deviation from the true path of freedom, independence, and happiness.

It was Locke's absolute belief that reason—the ability of human beings to make moral judgments—was as much a part of human nature as desire and emotion. Babies and children, he understood, could not use their power of reason until they were educated in the right way to do so. For Locke, the only right way of educating people was to instill in them the habit of thinking for themselves. Any ideas, principles, or beliefs that a person did not judge by his or her own intelligence should be rejected. The evidence of a person's own experience was the only evidence that Locke accepted as the material a person could use to formulate new ideas and, therefore, derive true knowledge.

Locke often used the candle as a symbol of the enlightening power of reason. As a religious person, he might have had in mind a verse from the Bible, Proverbs 20:27. It reads, "The spirit of man is the candle of the Lord." In other words, within every human being there is the candlelight of reason to guide him or her. It is a universal power that can lead to a universal understanding among people of different cultures, beliefs, and social status. In book 4,

Dessiné Par Desrais   Gravé par Carré

LA RAISON

chapter 20 of *An Essay Concerning Human Understanding*, Locke writes that rich and poor alike might equally be "confined to narrowness of Thought," but that everyone has the capacity to think for themselves. Whatever the different circumstances of people's lives, they have equal liberty to think according to their own minds.

For Locke, and, in fact, for all Enlightenment philosophers, the most important human faculty of all was reason. But what did Locke mean by reason? He explains his definition as follows:

> The word reason in the English language has different significations [meanings] . . . But the consideration I shall have of it here . . . is, as it stands for a faculty [ability] in man . . . whereby man is . . . distinguished from beasts, and wherein it

This engraving by Carre, after an original by Claude Louis Desrais, celebrates the human power of reason. It shows a woman who, with the light of reason in her hand, has command over nature, represented by a lion and a snake. Locke expressed supreme confidence of the power of reason. He insisted that everyone should be free to reason independently without fear of being punished by governments and religious authorities.

is evident he much surpasses [is superior to] them.

Reason, then, as Locke uses the word, is the faculty, or ability, in humans that makes them different from other animals. But Locke also says "it is the understanding that sets man above the rest of sensible beings [other animals]." What, then, is the difference between "understanding" and "reason"? Locke says "understanding" is like "a closet wholly shut from light, with only some little opening left, to let in external visible resemblances, or ideas of things without [from outside]." So "understanding" is like the mind: an empty chamber at birth that fills up with ideas during a person's life. It has the power of perception, but its contents have to be processed by the power of reason.

According to Locke, reason is our faculty to make judgments about the ideas we have in our minds. It is a kind of intellect, a power, that only humans have. Animals make judgments by their natural instinct for survival. Humans use their powers of reasoning to make moral judgments. Locke says that humans can also make more natural, instinctive judgments, like animals, but judgment by the use of reason sets humans apart from other animals. Reason, the power of humans to make moral judgments, is the supreme authority among all human faculties. Accordingly, he says, "Reason must be our last judge and guide in everything."

TRUTH

Locke loved truth. For him it was a reflection of the guiding light of reason. The love of truth was the same as the love of virtue and rejection of evil. The pursuit of truth led toward freedom from the influences of other people's opinions, principles, and beliefs—what Locke called prejudices. But Locke passionately believed that whatever a person believed in, whatever truths held dear by the guiding light and power of his or her intelligence, should not be imposed on others. Everyone, he believed, had the freedom and power to discover their own way in life—their own truths—based on the evidence of their own experiences. Locke believed that no matter how much a person believed in the truth of his or her own convictions, it was evil to impose those beliefs on another.

The imposition of a person's beliefs (truths) on another person was, for Locke, like the tyranny of kings who claimed a divine right to impose their power over their subjects. Tyranny, for Locke, was evil. It destroyed people's freedom. It denied people their right to think for themselves, to pursue their own route to happiness, and to be free to determine the direction of their lives. Locke believed that people must be tolerant of other people's beliefs. No one, he said, could be so absolutely right about their own beliefs that they had a right to impose those beliefs on others. It was more important, he said, to improve our own knowledge and intellect than impose our beliefs on others. This was the side of Locke's philosophy that showed his understanding and toleration of people's imperfections. He wrote in *An Essay Concerning Human Understanding*:

> We should do well to commiserate [have sympathy for] our mutual ignorance, and endeavour to remove it in all the gentle and fair ways of information; and not instantly treat others ill, as obstinate [stubborn] and perverse, because they will not renounce their own, and receive our opinions . . . For where is the man, that has uncontestable evidence of the truth of all that he holds [believes], or of the falsehood

of all he condemns? . . . The necessity of believing, without knowledge . . . often upon very slight grounds . . . should make us more busy and careful to inform ourselves, than constrain [impose upon] others.

We should, Locke said, love truth not for the sake of love, an emotion, but for the validity of truth itself, which was rational. Locke meant by this that a person's love of truth should be the desire to determine whether something is true. Anything a person accepts as being true that is not justified by the evidence of his or her own experience is "conceit, fancy, extravagance, any thing rather than understanding"—in other words, an illusion of truth. Anything a person believes to be true that is not judged by his or her intelligence, Locke said, is an imposition—a restraint—on his or her understanding that keeps it from being free. People can only be free, according to Locke, when they use their power of reason to think for themselves.

FREEDOM OF THOUGHT

Freedom of thought was the supreme freedom for Locke. It was the one freedom above all others that we should be careful not to impose upon, either in

The Martyrdom *of* T.Lofeby, H.Ramfey, T.Thirtell, Marg
Agnes Stanley, *in* Smithfield .

John Locke was particularly troubled by religious intolerance. He lived in an era when people were widely and often brutally persecuted for their religious beliefs. This engraving portrays a group of prominent Protestants being burned in London, England, during the sixteenth-century reign of the Catholic queen Mary I.

de, and

ourselves or in others. The most dangerous tyranny of all, for Locke, was a person's determination to impose prejudices on his or her own self. Anything not judged by a person's own reason was a restraint on his or her freedom of thought. It was Locke's belief that the most dangerous tyrant—the only one who could impose upon the freedom of one's own understanding, "that part [of us] which ought with the greatest care to be kept free from all imposition"—is oneself. He explains in *Of the Conduct of the Understanding*:

> In these two things, namely, an equal indifferency for [detachment from] all truth, I mean the receiving it in the love of it as truth, but not loving it for any other reason before we know it to be true, and in the examination of our principles, and not receiving any for such nor building on them till we are

Entitled *In the Sign of Minerva* (A l'Egide de Minerve), this allegorical painting by Leonard Defrance de Liege presents a powerful connection between reason and tolerance. An accompanying description reads, "In the sign of Minerva, Goddess of Reason, a golden age of tolerance unites people of different creeds, permits travel and the dissemination of books and newspapers."

fully convinced, as rational creatures, of their solidity, truth, and certainty, consists that freedom of the understanding which is necessary to a rational creature, and without which it is not truly an understanding. It is conceit, fancy, extravagance [i.e., an illusion], any thing rather than understanding, if it must be under the constraint of [if it is controlled by] receiving and holding opinions by the authority of any thing but their own . . . perceived evidence. This was rightly called imposition, and is of all other the worst and most dangerous sort of it. For we impose upon ourselves, which is the strongest imposition of all others; and we impose upon ourselves in that part which ought with the greatest care to be kept free from all imposition [i.e., our understanding].

Ultimately, Locke believed, it was the individual's responsibility to choose whether to be a tyrant or a liberator of his or her mind. Most people, Locke believed, allowed their prejudices and emotions to rule their lives in a kind of enslavement of their understanding. The power of human reason, he said, gave them the guarantee of being able to choose liberation.

THE INFLUENCE AND IMPORTANCE OF LOCKE'S IDEAS

1
2
3
4
5

CHAPTER 6

Locke's most famous work, *An Essay Concerning Human Understanding*, became a classic during the few remaining years of Locke's life. It was used as a university textbook. In 1700, it was translated into French, and, in 1701, into Latin. In the eighteenth century it was republished more than twenty times. Locke's stature was equal almost to Newton's in the fields of philosophical and scientific discovery. Locke's philosophy was a foundation of the eighteenth-century thinking about the nature of the universe as a huge machine of different parts, with humankind as a small cog in the mechanism. Other philosophers before Locke (Thomas Hobbes (1588–1679), for example) had proposed that human beings were a part of nature, rather

Thomas Hobbes was a great English philosopher of the seventeenth century. He believed that social order should be based on cooperation instead of ruling authority. Nevertheless, he argued that, once established, the social contract between people and its government could not be broken, thereby making the power of government absolute. John Locke strongly disagreed with this position.

than separate from nature, and could be explained in natural terms. Locke's philosophy proposed, first, that humans could be examined scientifically just like anything else in nature, and second, that they had a unique power—the power of reason—to dominate nature and gain mastery over it.

Although John Locke was not the first empiricist philosopher, he was the first of the so-called British Empiricists. The other two most important British Empiricists after Locke were George Berkeley (1685–1753) and the Scottish philosopher David Hume (1711–1776). As a student, Berkeley studied Locke's philosophy. He later criticized it in his own works. The title of Berkeley's major work, *A Treatise Concerning the Principles of Human Knowledge*, is similar to Locke's *An Essay Concerning Human Understanding*. Hume was most interested in the philosophy of human nature. The title of Hume's most important work, *A Treatise of Human Nature*, which he later rewrote and retitled *An Enquiry Concerning Human Understanding*, also echoed Locke. The philosophies of both Hume and Berkeley were linked to Locke's philosophy of the mind. Locke believed that the only way people could know about the outside world was the way they perceived it in their minds. Both Hume and Berkeley were philosophical skeptics, meaning that they thought that the mind was limited in what it could know about the outside world. Locke, in that sense, was also a skeptic, in that he believed that one could never know the real essence of things in the outside world. The only true knowledge, according to Locke, came from the relationships of ideas within the minds.

The branch of philosophy known as epistemology (the study of knowledge) goes back to the earliest classical philosophers. Locke's ideas about the subject were based on his belief

David Hume was a Scottish historian and philosopher of the eighteenth century. He wrote his greatest work, *The Treatise of Human Nature*, by the time he was twenty-five. The book was not well received when it was first published. Today, it is considered one of the most important works in British philosophy.

that the origin of all knowledge was a person's perception of the world through the senses. Locke's empirical approach to the theory of knowledge stimulated philosophical debate about the subject among eighteenth-century philosophers. Berkeley and Hume developed the empirical position in different ways.

Other important writers on the subject included Joseph Priestley, David Hartley, Francis Hutcheson, and Étienne Condillac. Locke's empiricism peaked in the philosophy of the great nineteenth-century British philosopher John Stuart Mill.

In Locke's time, psychology and psychoanalysis, which look into the reasons for human behavior, did not exist separate from philosophy. Locke was one of the first to try to answer questions about the mind and human actions from an empirical point of view. The experience of the mind and human behavior that Locke investigated were seeds later cultivated into the specialized areas of both psychology and psychoanalysis.

One of Locke's key philosophical principles was that everyone's ultimate goal was happiness. A philosophy derived from that principle in the eighteenth century was utilitarianism. The early utilitarians believed that pleasure was the greatest good and pain the greatest evil in human existence. Like Locke, they believed that all human beings were motivated by the pursuit of happiness and the avoidance of pain. Whatever produced the greatest happiness for the greatest number of people, according to the utilitarianists, was morally good. The main difference with Locke's philosophy was that utilitarianists measured good and evil relative to the greatest number of people it affected. Locke's philosophy, broadly, related more to individuals.

A GIANT OF THE ENLIGHTENMENT

Currents of Locke's philosophy run through the philosophy of other Enlightenment thinkers. These include the central importance of experience, the supreme authority of reason, the possibility for humans to dominate nature, and the use of scientific method to discover philosophical truths. Locke's greatest contribution to later centuries, however, was that he packaged his philosophy in human terms that people could easily understand and, more important, use in their own lives. He despised the confusion other writers created by dressing up their writings with sophisticated words that most people could not understand. The philosophy Locke presents in *An Essay Concerning Human Understanding* is not always easy to follow, but he published it, as he says in the "Epistle to the Reader," "with hopes [that] it may be useful to others."

The most important political use of Locke's philosophy was in the founding principles of the United States of America. Many of the liberal principles on which the United States was founded

Entitled *Washington Crossing the Delaware, 1776*, this painting is an artist's representation of a scene from the American Revolution. In rebelling against England, the American colonies did what Locke's philosophy encourages people to do when their government breaks the social contract—overthrow it.

echo the philosophy of John Locke. Abraham Lincoln said in a speech in 1863 that "this nation, under God, shall have a new birth of freedom; and that government of the people, by the people, and for the people, shall not perish from the earth."

The freedom of people to determine their government was an important concept of Locke's "Second Treatise on Civil Government."

Locke's political philosophy was also clearly reflected in the first paragraph of the Declaration of Independence. The declaration reflects Locke's philosophy of human equality, happiness, and government by consent of the majority. Locke believed, as the Declaration of Independence repeated, that those rights were "self-evident" and given to all human beings by "their Creator." In the first draft of the declaration, Thomas Jefferson copied Locke's phrase "life, liberty, and property." This was later changed to "life, liberty, and the pursuit of happiness."

Not only do people have an "unalienable" (absolute) right to life, liberty, and the pursuit of happiness, they have, as Locke said, an obligation to overthrow any government that "becomes destructive of these ends." Rebellion, according to Locke's "Second Treatise on Civil Government,"

A Declaration by the Representatives of the UNITED STATES OF AMERICA, in General Congress assembled.

When in the course of human events it becomes necessary for one people to dissolve the political bands which have connected them with another, and to assume among the powers of the earth the separate and equal station to which the laws of nature & of nature's god entitle them, a decent respect to the opinions of mankind requires that they should declare the causes which impel them to the separation.

We hold these truths to be self-evident, that all men are created equal, that they are endowed by their creator with equal creation they derive rights inherent & inalienable, among which are the preservation of life, & liberty, & the pursuit of happiness; that to secure these ends, governments are instituted among men, deriving their just powers from the consent of the governed; that whenever any form of government becomes destructive of these ends, it is the right of the people to alter or to abolish it, & to institute new government, laying it's foundation on such principles & organising it's powers in such form, as to them shall seem most likely to effect their safety & happiness. prudence indeed will dictate that governments long established should not be changed for light & transient causes: and accordingly all experience hath shewn that mankind are more disposed to suffer while evils are sufferable, than to right themselves by abolishing the forms to which they are accustomed. but when a long train of abuses & usurpations [begun at a distinguished period, & pursuing invariably the same object, evinces a design to subject reduce them under absolute despotism] it is their right, it is their duty, to throw off such government, & to provide new guards for their future security. such has been the patient sufferance of these colonies; & such is now the necessity which constrains them to expunge their former systems of government. the history of his present majesty is a history of unremitting injuries and usurpations, among which appears no solitary fact to contradict the uniform tenor of the rest, all of which have in direct object the establishment of an absolute tyranny over these states. to prove this, let facts be submitted to a candid world, [for the truth of which we pledge a faith yet unsullied by falsehood.]

was a legitimate way to overthrow a tyrannical government if that government threatened the "liberties and properties" of its citizens. The separation of the powers of the executive (the president or ruler), legislative (Congress or Parliament), and the judicial (the justice system) branches of a nation, which Locke also proposed in the treatise, is also a basic concept in the Constitution of the United States.

The most enduring aspect of Locke's works is what he had to say about the conduct of human lives, that we fall short of our potential and how we can aim higher. Locke reminds us about principles that transcend his philosophy: truth, freedom, toleration, common sense, and charity toward others. Locke's insight into those human concerns continues to enlighten us more than three centuries after his death.

The United States' Founding Fathers were inspired by the philosophy of John Locke in both rebelling against English rule and in establishing a system of government in the new nation. Pictured here are the original draft of the Declaration of Independence and Thomas Jefferson, its author, who borrowed the phrase "life, liberty, and property" directly from Locke.

A PHILOSOPHER OF LASTING IMPORTANCE

Locke was important because he was original. He was a revolutionary thinker who opposed the tyrannies of prejudice, dogma, opinion, and ignorance. Despite all its flaws, his philosophy has inspired and stimulated others to think and act in pursuit of their own truths. Three hundred years after his death, the light of Locke's wisdom and humanity continues to shine. In *An Outline of Philosophy*, the great twentieth-century philosopher Bertrand Russell summed up Locke's importance as follows:

> Locke was a contemporary and friend of [Sir Isaac] Newton; his [Locke's] great book, "An Essay Concerning Understanding," was published at about the same time as Newton's "Principia." His influence has been enormous, greater, in fact, than his abilities would seem to warrant; and this influence was not only philosophical, but quite as much political and social. He was one of the creators of eighteenth century liberalism: democracy, religious toleration, freedom of economic enterprise, educational progress, all owe much to him. The English Revolution of

1688 embodied his ideas; the American Revolution of 1776 and the French Revolution of 1789 expressed what had grown, in a century, out of his teachings. And in all these movements, philosophy and politics went hand in hand. Thus the practical success of Locke's ideas has been extraordinary.

Locke was not the greatest philosopher of the Enlightenment. He had then, and continues to have now, many critics. His method of critical reasoning, how-

This nineteenth-century vase from the St. Petersburg Imperial Porcelain Factory bears a portrait of John Locke, painted after an original by Sir Godfrey Kneller.

ever, was revolutionary. It requires us to turn inside out and question and examine everything we know or believe. We should never be afraid, Locke said, to

This is the terra-cotta model of a full-length marble statue of John Locke at Christ Church College in Oxford, England. The figure, set in a pensive pose, holds a large, impressive book, which is a symbol of Locke's influential role as an original philosopher.

look inside ourselves to question and, if necessary, reject any beliefs and principles that, on the evidence of our experience and by the power of our reason, we discover to be false. We should never be afraid to let go of false principles and opinions and prejudices. We should never be afraid, in short, to be revolutionaries.

Locke was a philosopher of human nature. He observed the shortcomings and imperfections of human beings with a sympathetic eye. Strands of human nature, in all their different colors and patterns, are woven through the tapestry of Locke's philosophy. He understood people's weaknesses, illusions, and delusions. He recognized the power of irrational human emotions. His philosophy was empirical, derived from the observation and experience of human behavior. It was the philosophy of the universal human condition, that people everywhere and in all times struggle to be free from the binds of their imperfections. The reason why Locke is still important today is that we recognize in ourselves what he says in his philosophy about human behavior, about the universal human aspirations for freedom and happiness, and the constant moral dilemma of choosing the path of our own destiny.

TIMELINE

1603–1714	The Stewarts reign in England.
1603	James I rises to the English throne.
1620	Pilgrims sail to America.
1625	Charles I becomes king of England.
1632	John Locke is born on August 29 at Wrington, Somerset, in the west of England.
1642–1651	The English Civil War takes place.
1649	Charles I is executed.
1649–1653	England goes through the period of the commonwealth.
1653–1659	England is a protectorate, with Oliver Cromwell serving as lord protector until he dies in 1658.
1660	The monarchy is restored with Charles II (1660–1685)
1683	Locke goes to Holland to escape persecution in England.
1685	The reign of James II begins.
1687	Sir Isaac Newton's *Principia* is published.
1688	The Glorious Revolution takes place.

1689	Locke returns to England from self-imposed exile in Holland.
1690	The first version of Locke's *An Essay Concerning Human Understanding* is published.
1702–1714	Queen Anne rises to the English throne.
1704	John Locke dies at Oates, Essex, on October 28, 1704.

GLOSSARY

abhor To hate.

aspirations Hopes, ambitions, aims.

atheist Someone who does not believe in God.

communion The act of coming together.

contemporary Someone living at the same time, generally of the same age.

deduce To reach a conclusion by logical steps.

deviation Straying from a specific direction or path.

dogma Established principles or ideas.

dogmatic Intolerant of other principles or ideas.

dynastic Of a dynasty or line of rulers from the same family.

empirical Perceived by the senses (sight, taste, smell, touch, hearing).

empiricism The theory that human knowledge is based only on the experiences of our senses.

epistemology The science of the study of knowledge.

heresy Rejection of commonly held beliefs or truths.

overweening Arrogant or conceited.

pedantic Sticking precisely and literally to an idea or principle.

phenomena Plural of phenomenon, anything perceived by observation or other empirical knowledge.

pragmatic Practical, down-to-earth.

prevailing Being in force or current at the time.

rationality The quality of being logical, using one's reason.

rhetoric The art of oration (making speeches).

skeptic One who questions or doubts the truth of something.

sovereignty An authority or supreme power.

transcend To rise above, surpass, go beyond.

tyrant An absolute ruler, dictator.

uncontestable Cannot be denied or argued against.

warrant Justify, deserve.

FOR MORE INFORMATION

American Philosophical Association
University of Delaware
31 Amstel Avenue
Newark, DE 19716-4797
(302) 831-1112
Web site: http://www.apa.udel.
  edu/apa

John Locke Foundation
200 West Morgan Street
Raleigh, NC 27601
(919) 828-3876
Web site: http://www.johnlocke.org

The Locke Institute
4084 University Drive, Suite 103
Fairfax, VA 22030-6812
(703) 934-6934
Web site: http://www.
  thelockeinstitute.org

Philosopher's Information Center
1616 East Wooster Street, Suite 34
Bowling Green, OH 43402
(419) 353-8830
Web site: http://www.philinfo.org

WEB SITES

Due to the changing nature of Internet links, the Rosen Publishing Group, Inc., has developed an online list of Web sites related to the subject of this book. This site is updated regularly. Please use this link to access the list:

http://www.rosenlinks.com/phen/jolo

For Further Reading

Aaron, Richard I. *John Locke.* Oxford, England: Clarendon Press, 1971.

Cranston, Maurice. *John Locke: A Biography.* Oxford, England: Oxford University Press, 1985.

Grant, Ruth W. *John Locke's Liberalism.* Chicago, IL: University of Chicago Press, 1991.

Honderich, Ted, ed. *The Oxford Companion to Philosophy.* Oxford, England: Oxford University Press, 1995.

Jenkins, John J. *Understanding Locke: An Introduction to Philosophy Through John Locke's Essay.* Edinburgh, Scotland: Edinburgh University Press, 1985.

O'Connor, D. J. *John Locke.* Middlesex, England: Penguin Books, 1952.

Porter, Roy. *Studies in European History—The Enlightenment.* New York, NY: Palgrave, 2001.

Russell, Bertrand. *An Outline of Philosophy.* London, England: George Allen & Unwin Ltd., 1932.

Yolton, John W. *John Locke and the Way of Ideas.* Oxford, England: Clarendon Press, 1956.

Yolton, Jean, and John Yolton. *John Locke: A Reference Guide.* Boston, MA: G. K. Hall, 1985.

BIBLIOGRAPHY

Aaron, Richard I. *John Locke.* Oxford, England: Clarendon Press, 1971.

Bourne, Henry Richard Fox. *The Life of John Locke.* Bristol, England: Thoemmes Press, 1991.

King, Lord William Peter. *The Life and Letters of John Locke.* London, England: George Bell & Sons, 1884.

King, Lord William Peter. *The Life of John Locke: With Extracts from His Correspondence, Journals, and Common-place Books.* Bristol, England: Thoemmes Press, 1991.

Locke, John. *An Essay Concerning Human Understanding.* London, England: Penguin Classics, Penguin Books, 1997.

Locke, John. *Some Thoughts Concerning Education.* Edited by John W. Yolton and Jean S. Yolton. Oxford, England: Oxford University Press, 1989.

Locke, John. *Some Thoughts Concerning Education and of the Conduct of the Understanding.* Edited by Ruth W. Grant and Nathan Tarcov. Indianapolis, IN: Hackett Publishing Co., Inc., 1996.

Locke, John. *Two Treatises of Government.* Edited by Peter Laslett. Cambridge, England: Cambridge University Press, 1960.

Russell, Bertrand. *History of Western Philosophy.* London, England: Unwin Paperbacks, 1979.

Russell, Bertrand. *An Outline of Philosophy.* London, England: George Allen & Unwin Ltd., 1932.

Schouls, Peter A. *Reasoned Freedom: John Locke and Enlightenment.* Ithaca, NY: Cornell University Press, 1992.

INDEX

A

Act for Regulation of Printing, 31
American Revolution, 95
Aquinas, Saint Thomas, 42
Aristotle, 25, 38, 53, 55, 65, 68

B

Bacon, Sir Francis, 56–58, 59
Berkeley, George, 86, 87
Bernier, François, 29
Bourne, Fox, 59
Boyle, Robert, 10, 26, 68, 69
Brahe, Tycho, 65, 66

C

Charles I, King, 18, 20, 23
Charles II, King, 17, 20, 21,
    28, 29
Christ Church College (Oxford
    University), 25, 53, 68
Clarke, Edward, 46
"Collected Papers," 38
Collins, Anthony, 9
Condillac, Étienne, 88
Copernicus, Nicolaus, 65, 66,
    67, 68
  heliocentric theory, 65, 67
Council of Trade and
    Plantations, 28
Cromwell, Oliver, 20

D

Declaration of
  Independence, 91
deductive reasoning,
  56–57, 62
Descartes, René, 17, 59–64,
  66, 68
Discourse on Method, 63

E

empiricism, 58–59, 62, 65,
  68, 69, 86, 87–88, 97
England in the seventeenth
  century, 10, 13, 17–23
 and Catholicism, 18, 20, 21
 civil war of, 18
 politics of, 18–23
 and Protestantism, 13, 18,
  20, 21, 23
 religious conflict, 10,
  17–23
 revolution of, 94–95
 science, 10–11
 wars, 10
Enlightenment philosophy,
  7, 9, 38, 55–56, 75,
  89, 95
*Enquiry Concerning Human
  Understanding, An, (A
  Treatise Concerning the
  Principles of Human
  Knowledge)*, 86
epistemology, 37, 87
"Epistle to the Reader," 11,
  15, 32, 37, 38, 69, 89
 objective of, 38

*Essay Concerning Human
  Understanding, An*, 12,
  32–52, 61–62, 75, 78–79,
  84, 89, 94
 Book 1 ("Of Innate
  Notions"), 35, 37
 Book 2 ("Of Ideas"), 35
 Book 3 ("Of Words"), 35
 Book 4 ("Of Knowledge
  and Opinion"), 35
 definition of philosophy, 11
 objective of, 37, 89
 origins of, 32–34

F

Filmer, Sir Robert, 39, 41
French Revolution, 95

G

Galilei, Galileo, 10, 66–67, 68
Gassendi, Pierre, 29,
  64, 68
Glorious Revolution, 23,
  31, 41

H

Herbert, Thomas, (Earl of
  Pembroke), 35–37
*History of Western
  Philosophy*, 15, 38
Hobbes, Thomas, 84
Holland in seventeenth
  century, 13, 14–17
 and Catholicism, 13
 and politics, 21–23

and Protestantism, 13, 15, 17
and science, 15
Hume, David, 86, 87
Hutcheson, Francis, 88
Huygens, Christian, 15, 69

I

inductive reasoning, 57–58, 59, 64
Instauratio Magna, 56

J

James II, King, 21–23, 30, 31
Jefferson, Thomas, 91

K

Kepler, Johannes, 66
King, Lord Peter, 10, 25, 30, 51

L

Leeuwenhoek, Antoni van, 15
Letter Concerning Toleration, 39
Life of John Locke, The, 59
Lincoln, Abraham, 90
Locke, John
  birth/childhood of, 12, 18, 24
  on civil liberty, 28
  on community, 43–45
  death of, 31

education of, 10, 24–26, 29–30, 53, 70, 73
on education, 46–51, 52
on emotions, 70–73, 79, 83, 97
family of, 18, 24, 51
in France, 28–29
on freedom of thought, 79–83
on government, 12
on happiness, 11, 53, 71, 73, 78, 88, 91, 97
in Holland, 17, 29, 31, 34, 46
on human nature, 70, 71, 73, 97
influence of, 7–9, 12, 84–97
influences on, 24, 53–69
on innate ideas, 61–62, 64
on knowledge, 11, 37, 47, 48, 55, 78, 87
legal troubles of, 29–31
in London, England, 32
on natural law, 41–42, 43
on nature, 37–38
in Oates, England, 31, 34, 59
in Oxford, England, 26, 29–30, 68
on reason, 9, 10, 11, 37, 38, 42, 43, 47, 48, 50, 51, 55, 62, 70, 71, 72, 73, 75–77, 79, 81, 83, 86
religion of, 28
on sensory perception, 53
on social contract, 44, 45
on "state of nature," 41–43

on toleration, 9, 10, 28,
    39, 78, 93
on truth, 9, 11, 38, 58,
    77–79, 93
on tyranny, 77–78, 81, 82
on understanding, 76,
    79, 82
work of, 26, 28
Louis XIV, 20

M

Maria, Henrietta, 18
Mary II, Queen, 23, 31
Masham, Lady, 31, 59
Mill, John Stuart, 88

N

Newton, Isaac, 10, 67–68,
    69, 84, 94
Novum Organum, 59

O

*Of the Conduct of the
    Understanding*, 48,
    51–52, 81–83
Of Truth, 58
*Outline of Philosophy,
    An*, 94

P

*Patriarcha; or, The Natural
    Power of Kings*, 39
Penn, William, 30
Peterborough, Earl of, 11
philosophical skeptics,
    86–87

*Posthumous Works of Mr.
    John Locke*, 51
Priestley, Joseph, 88
Principia, 68, 94
Puritans, 17–18

R

*Reasonableness of
    Christianity, The*, 51
reductionism, 63–64
Royal Society, 20, 26
Russell, Bertrand, 15, 38, 94
Ryle, Gilbert, 38

S

Shaftesbury, Earl of (Lord
    Ashley), 28–31, 32
*Some Thoughts Concerning
    Education*, 46, 47–48,
    50, 52
Swammerdam, Jan, 15
Sydenham, Thomas, 69

T

Thirty Years' War, 14
Toleration Act, 31
*Two Treatises of Govern-
    ment*, 12, 39–46, 93
    "First Treatise," 39–41
    "Second Treatise," 41–46,
    91–93

W

Westminster School, 24, 53
William of Orange, 21–23,
    31, 41

About the Author

Graham Faiella is a writer, researcher, and editor who has authored several books for young adults on historical literature, nutrition, fishing, and whales. He comes to this project with a great fascination for the revolutionary spirit of the Enlightenment thinkers and the philosophy of John Locke, in particular. Originally from Bermuda, Mr. Faiella has lived in London, England, since graduating with an MA in Italian and Hispanic Studies from Edinburgh University in 1978.

Credits

Designer: Evelyn Horovicz
Editor: Wayne Anderson
Photo Researcher: Amy Feinberg